TUPAC SHAKUR
An Eternal Legacy

By

Morghan Knight

Table of Contents

Introduction

Tupac Amaru Shakur is a name that echoes through the corridors of hip-hop history with a power that few others can match. His music, art, and activism have transcended mere music to become a force of social commentary, a platform for self-expression, and a catalyst for change. Tupac's life was a whirlwind of contradictions, a kaleidoscope of brilliance and tumult, and a relentless quest for truth.

Born into poverty and inequality, Tupac's early years were marked by struggle and adversity. Yet, he had a spark—an incandescent talent that would set the world ablaze. As a rapper, he was a lyrical maestro, weaving intricate narratives of his experiences on the mean streets of East Harlem and Baltimore. His words resonated with the disenfranchised, the marginalized, and the oppressed, speaking truth to power and amplifying the voices of the voiceless.

But Tupac was more than just a rapper. He was a poet, a philosopher, an actor, an activist, and a provocateur. He challenged the establishment, questioned societal norms, and exposed the fissures in a nation grappling with racial tension and economic disparity. His art was a mirror reflecting the harsh realities of the world around him, and he refused to look away, even when the glare became blinding.

This biography seeks to unravel the complex tapestry of Tupac's life—a life that burned brightly and was extinguished far too soon. Through research, interviews with those who knew him best, and an exploration of his music, films, and writings, we aim to shed light on the enigmatic figure who continues to captivate and inspire millions around the world.

Chapter 1

A Star is Born

On the evening of June 16, 1971, a star was born in the dimly illuminated hallways of New York City's Harlem Hospital. Tupac Amaru Shakur was born with a name rich in meaning and history. His given name, Tpac Amaru II, was a reference to a revolutionary who battled for justice in Peru in the 18th century and was named for the revolutionary Tpac Amaru II. His name carries the weight of the aspirations of his mother, Afeni Shakur, a Black Panther activist herself.

Tupac's upbringing was far from luxurious. Raised in East Harlem, a district known for its poverty and crime, he was exposed to the harsh realities of inner-city life from a young age. His family's struggles were emblematic of the difficulties faced by many African Americans in the 1970s and '80s—a period when economic disparity and systemic racism had a profound impact on their prospects.

The Shakur family's life was characterized by frequent relocation. Tupac's mother, Afeni, had difficulty making ends meet, often moving from one low-income area to another in search of stability. It was during these formative years that Tupac began to recognize the injustices that surrounded him. The turbulence of his early life would later become a source of motivation for his music and activism.

Tupac's upbringing was characterized by a combination of factors that molded his outlook. His mother, Afeni, was a devoted member of the Black Panther Party, introducing him to political activism and social awareness from a young age. Her dedication to the civil rights movement and her participation in the fight for racial justice left a lasting impression on her son, sowing the seeds of his later activism.

In addition to his mother's influence, Tupac was also inspired by the arts. His family's involvement in theater acquainted him with the realm of acting and performance, sparking a love of storytelling that would later be reflected in his songs and on the big screen. These two forces—activism and the arts—converged in Tupac's life in a way that shaped his unique journey.

As Tupac matured, his early interests and talents began to coalesce into a formidable power. He started to write poetry and rap lyrics as a way to express himself and to escape from the harsh realities of his environment. His natural aptitude for words became increasingly evident, and he sharpened his skills as a wordsmith, taking inspiration from the struggles he saw and the experiences he went through.

In the crucible of East Harlem, Tupac Shakur's identity as an artist and a social commentator began to take shape. He realized that his voice could be a potent tool for transformation, a medium through which he could not only tell his own story but also amplify the voices of those whose stories often went unheard. Little did he know that he was on the brink of a journey that would take him from the streets of Harlem to the peak of the music industry and, eventually, to the forefront of social and political discourse.

Chapter 2

Rise to Fame

The tumultuous atmosphere of East Harlem during Tupac Shakur's formative years created an ideal environment for the growth of a future star. As he faced the difficulties of his neighborhood, his natural talent and unyielding ambition began to set him apart from his peers. This period marked the beginning of his journey to becoming the renowned figure we know today.

Tupac's initial involvement in the music industry can be traced back to his time with the hip-hop group Digital

Underground. He joined the group in the late 1980s, initially as a backup dancer and rapper. Although this may have seemed like a humble start, it was the gateway to an industry that would soon be revolutionized by his presence. Digital Underground provided Tupac with invaluable experience and exposure, allowing him to hone his skills and find his own style within the rap community.

Tupac debuted as a recording artist in 1991 with the band Digital Underground on the song "Same Song." His ascent into the realm of professional music started with this. His lyrical talent and personality shone strongly even in these early days. This youthful performer immediately caught the attention of the crowds because to his or her captivating stage presence and undeniable air of authenticity.

But it didn't take Tupac long to go out on his own because of his need for creative freedom. In 1991, he released "2Pacalypse Now," his first solo album. The album received considerable attention for its realistic representation of the challenges experienced by African Americans in underprivileged neighborhoods, while not being an immediate economic success. Tupac's songs reflected the harsh reality of his own background and were frank, bold, and unashamedly hostile.

The movie "2Pacalypse Now" was not without criticism. Some people condemned it for having themes and explicit lyrics that addressed racial injustice and police violence. Tupac stood out as an artist because of his willingness to confront difficult issues, though. He utilized his music as a platform to speak out against the injustices he saw every day and to offer people who had been silenced by society a voice.

The release of "2Pacalypse Now" marked the emergence of Tupac Shakur as a socially conscious artist. His lyrics were a call to action, a demand for change, and a reflection of the frustrations and anger that many young African Americans felt. At a time when gangsta rap was becoming popular, Tupac's music was unique for its combination of street credibility and a strong dedication to tackling systemic issues.

As Tupac's solo career began to take off, it was evident that he was not just another rapper; he was a powerful presence. His magnetic personality and undeniable talent drew people from all walks of life into his circle. His ability to express the struggles of his generation resonated with a wide and varied audience, cementing his status as a soon-to-be cultural icon.

The groundwork was laid for a tale to emerge in East Harlem's furnace. The transition of Tupac Shakur from backup dancer to solo musician was just the start. His second album, "Strictly 4 My N.I.G.G.A.Z.," would increase his notoriety and pave the way for a career that would go beyond music and have a lasting impression on society.

Chapter 3

The Controversial Icon

As Tupac Shakur's popularity in the hip-hop community grew, controversy surrounded his life story more and more. The intricate network of legal issues, disputes, and rivalries that would come to define this mysterious artist is explored in Chapter 3 of his biography.

Numerous legal disputes and run-ins with the law characterized Tupac's ascent to fame and notoriety. Adversity had already moulded his early years, but fame presented its own set of difficulties.

Tupac frequently attracted the attention of law enforcement because of his combative lyrics and persona, and he soon found himself in a number of legal disputes that would cast a shadow over his career.

The historic Quad Studios shooting in New York City in 1994 was one of the most significant events that occurred during this time. Tupac was ambushed and shot several times; this incident had a significant impact on both his life and the course of hip-hop history. Theories and rumors are still circulating today about the shooting's circumstances, which are still clouded in mystery and dispute.

Tupac's life changed after the incident at Quad Studios. It fueled the rivalry between the West Coast and East Coast hip-hop scenes, which would later come to define a period in the history of music. Tupac felt that his murder had been planned by people with connections to East Coast musicians, intensifying the rivalry between the two coasts. This conflict would have far-reaching effects and ultimately contribute to Tupac's premature death.

Conflicts and feuds, both actual and imagined, were a constant feature of Tupac's existence. He got into conflicts with Notorious B.I.G., Sean Combs (P. Diddy), and Bad Boy Records, among other well-known musicians. Diss recordings and public jeers were a defining feature of this hip-hop period as a result of the frequent spillover of these confrontations into their music. Particularly, the bitter rivalry between Biggie Smalls and Tupac would come to symbolize the East Coast-West Coast conflict, with catastrophic results for both musicians.

The East Coast-West Coast rivalry was a heavy cloud over the hip-hop scene in the middle of the 1990s. It was propelled by a toxic mix of rivalry, ego, and, in some instances, actual hostility. Sensationalizing the feud in the media only served to inflame hostilities, creating an atmosphere of dread and uncertainty among hip-hop artists. Tupac was the eye of the storm because of his blunt and aggressive personality.

Chapter 4

Artistic Evolution

This Chapter explores a crucial phase in his life and career, a time when his artistic development, personal development, and the publication of important albums helped to establish his status as a cultural icon.

One of the most important turning points in Tupac's career was the release of "Me Against the World." The album, which was released in 1995 while he was incarcerated, showed the rapper at his more sensitive and introspective best. It explored themes of love, sorrow, and the hardships of a young black man in America, which marked a change from his earlier, more aggressive work. One of the album's finest songs, "Dear Mama," is a moving ode to his mother, Afeni Shakur, and showcases his talent for fusing sincere feeling with literary skill.

When "Me Against the World" was released, Tupac was going through a difficult time in his life. He had plenty of time to contemplate because he was in jail and dealing with legal issues. Tupac's status as a successful artist continued to grow while he was behind bars. From behind bars, he wrote letters, poems, and songs, solidifying his reputation as a contemporary poet and social commentator. It's evident that he had the capacity to turn his experiences into moving words, and his fans were quite responsive to this.

Tupac was a different person after he got released from prison. He was now very conscious of the influence of his words and the results of his deeds. His devotion to tackling social issues in his music was a clear indication of this newly acquired consciousness. Tupac's music had developed into a forum for commentary on the larger issues black communities in America were confronting. It was no longer merely a reflection of his own experiences.

In 1996, Tupac's career reached a pinnacle with the release of **"All Eyez on Me"**. This double album was a tour de force, displaying his lyrical skill, storytelling ability, and magnetic personality. It included hits such as **"California Love," "How Do U Want It,"** and "Ambitionz Az a Ridah," confirming Tupac's status as a bona fide superstar. The album's success demonstrated his capacity to bridge the gap between the streets and the mainstream, appealing to a wide range of people while staying true to his origins.

However, **"All Eyez on Me"** was more than just a commercial success. It was a representation of Tupac's multifaceted identity—an artist, a provocateur, a poet, and a visionary. The album examined topics of fame, ambition, and the cost of success, all while upholding a dedication to addressing the social and political issues that still weighed heavily on Tupac's mind.

Chapter 5

The Activist & Philanthropist

Tupac Shakur was a multifaceted individual who was devoted to social activism and philanthropy. This chapter is a testament to this. We explore Tupac's strong commitment to social justice and his tireless efforts to make a positive difference in the world beyond music.

Tupac was more than just a rapper; he was a vocal proponent of change. His mother, Afeni, raised him with the values of the Black Panther movement, instilling in him a strong sense of social responsibility. Throughout his career,

Tupac used his platform to bring attention to issues such as racial injustice, police brutality, and the struggles of marginalized communities. His music became a powerful tool to amplify the voices of the oppressed and to challenge the existing power structures.

The vocal support Tupac showed for the Black Panther Party was one of the turning points in his development as an activist. A revolutionary group called the Panthers battled for the freedom and rights of black people in America. Tupac passionately embraced the Panthers' history while facing criticism and scrutiny for his affiliation with the organisation, of which his mother had been an active member.

Tupac was a passionate activist who used his influence and resources to engage in community outreach and philanthropy. In 1993, he established the Tupac Amaru Shakur Foundation, an organization devoted to providing arts and educational programs to underserved communities. Through initiatives such as the "Code Black" scholarship program and arts camps, Tupac sought to equip young people with the means to break free from the cycle of poverty and violence.

Throughout his career, Tupac was a vocal critic of the justice system and the mistreatment of black individuals by law enforcement. He used his music to address these issues, often drawing from his own experiences. Tracks like **"Trapped"** and **"Soulja's Story"** provided a scathing critique of police brutality and the pervasive racism that plagued American society. His ability to combine storytelling with social commentary made his message even more powerful.

Tupac's advocacy extended beyond his charitable work and the music studio. He participated in public discussion about racial and social inequalities using his platform. He took part in interviews and panel discussions where he bravely spoke about subjects that many famous people avoided. He attracted both admiration and criticism for his candor and unvarnished honesty, yet he persisted in his pursuit of justice regardless of the consequences.

Tupac gave a speech at a rally in 1992, following the Los Angeles riots brought on by the conviction of the police officers responsible for beating Rodney King, in which he fervently urged for unity among black communities. Those who were dissatisfied and disillusioned by institutional inequities found his views to be resonant. Tupac became a ray of hope and a figure of resistance because of his ability to express the rage and frustration of a generation.

Chapter 6

Tragic End

The last, most terrible period of Tupac Shakur's life—one characterized by the shooting in Las Vegas, the circumstances leading up to that awful night, the fallout, and the lingering questions surrounding his untimely death—is explored in Chapter 6 of his biography.

Tupac Shakur went to a boxing event at the MGM Grand Garden Arena in Las Vegas on the evening of September 7, 1996. He was among pals and taking in the exciting energy of the occasion. He had no idea how this night would change the path of his life and the hip-hop genre for all time.

There is still debate and conjecture around what exactly happened before the tragic shooting. The anxiety and unease around Tupac increased as a result of the numerous disputes and altercations he had in the weeks before. Tupac and his group were assaulted by unknown assailants in a drive-by shooting as they were leaving the MGM Grand on the night of the shooting. Tupac was struck numerous times and suffered serious wounds.

The shooting's aftermath rocked both the music business and the entire world.

Tupac was taken urgently to the hospital, where he would struggle for six days to stay alive. Tupac Shakur died at the age of 25 on September 13, 1996, despite the world's hopes for a miracle as they watched with baited breath.

The hip-hop scene and beyond were rocked by the news of Tupac's passing. A career that had blazed brightly but all too soon came to a tragic and premature end as a result. His death ushered in the end of an era in hip-hop and left a vacuum in the worlds of activism and music.

There is still a lot of discussion and passionate speculation about how Tupac was killed. Over the years, many hypotheses and conspiracies have surfaced, but the truth is still unclear. The identity of Tupac's killer or killers is still a mystery, as is the drive-by shooting in Las Vegas.

Along with his music, Tupac leaves behind a lasting legacy of unanswered questions and unsolved riddles. His influence on hip-hop, activism, and social conscience are still felt today, as is the remembrance of a captivating and nuanced musician who made a lasting impression on society.

Tupac's Killer Arrested

Duane Keith Davis claimed to have been a front-seat passenger in the vehicle from which another passenger fired the gunfire that murdered Tupac Shakur in 1998 when speaking to a cable station.

According to a former investigator who looked into the incident, Davis, also known as "Keffe D," confessed to police about his involvement in the case in 2009, but the information was not immediately put to use.

Davis, 60, was later detained in Las Vegas on Friday following what police claim was a renewed investigation, and a grand jury had indicted him in the case on counts of murder with a dangerous weapon. About 27 years have passed since the rapper was shot on the Las Vegas Strip as he was exiting a boxing match.

According to investigators, the September 7, 1996 shooting was a reprisal attack on the 25-year-old star. Authorities claim that after the rapper and others abused Davis' nephew that day, Davis quickly planned and executed the shooting.

According to authorities, Davis is the only suspect in the case who is still alive. A record label executive who was driving

Shakur is the other live witness, according to Davis, who claimed to be one of two in a memoir.

"Over the last five years, we've conducted countless interviews and corroborated numerous facts that were not only consistent with the crime scene on the night of the incident, but also corroborated and were consistent with the sequence of events that night," said Jason Johansson, a Las Vegas police homicide lieutenant, during a news conference on Friday.

Here is what we know about Davis, the circumstances surrounding the shooting, and his arrest and indictment.

Conclusion

Tupac Amaru Shakur's life was a whirlwind of brilliance, controversy, and tragedy. Raised in a challenging environment, he used his remarkable talents to transcend his circumstances and become a source of inspiration for many people who could relate to his lyrics and experiences. His music was a reflection of the harsh realities of inner-city life, police brutality, and systemic inequality, but it also served as a source of strength and a call to action.

Throughout his career, Tupac was not afraid to address difficult topics, from the struggles of his upbringing in East Harlem to the destructive effects of racial prejudice and violence. His words were direct, honest, and sometimes confrontational, but they resonated with a wide audience that found comfort and encouragement in his words.

He was a multidimensional artist who studied acting, poetry, and activism in addition to his work as a rapper. He frequently put his life and reputation at risk to speak out against injustice, using his prominence as a platform to promote social justice. His membership in the Black Panther Party and his involvement in charitable work and community outreach showed a strong desire to have a good impact on the world.

Tupac's life was not without controversy and hardship, and Chapter 6 provided details on the sad events that led to his untimely demise. His murder in Las Vegas is still one of the longest-running mysteries in the music and entertainment industries, leaving behind not only his songs but also a long list of unanswered questions and theories.

Tupac's influence has only increased in the years after his death. His influence on hip-hop is enormous, and new generations of fans continue to connect with his music. He is recognized not only as an artist but also as a representation of sincerity, resiliency, and the strength of individual expression.

Made in the USA
Middletown, DE
10 May 2024

54143944R00024